X Algorithm mastery

Disclaimer: The purpose of this copyright page is for
informational purposes only and does not constitute legal
advice. Please consult with an attorney for specific legal
advice.

X

ALGORITHM MASTERY

A thriving account, skyrocketing your impression and monetizing your x hustle

TABLE OF CONTENT

Introduction
- Unveiling the X Algorithm: Why It Matters and How It Works
- Your Roadmap to X Algorithm Mastery: What to Expect from This Book

Part 1: Cracking the X Code

Part 2: Skyrocketing Your Impressions

- Leveraging Collaborations: Co-creation, challenges, cross-promotion

(Image of two people high fiving on a laptop)

- o Power of Partnerships: Brand deals, sponsored content, influencer groups (Image of a handshake between two influencers)
- o Finding Your Tribe: Joining Communities and Networking (Image of a group of diverse people using the platform)

- o Seeking Guidance: Identifying and approaching potential mentors (Image of a person looking up at a silhouette of a successful person)

- o The Power of Mentorship: Learning from experience, receiving feedback, staying motivated (Image of a mentor and mentee having a conversation)

- o Building Your Support Network: Forming mastermind groups, finding accountability partners (Image of a group of people sitting in a circle, sharing ideas)

- o Affiliate Marketing
- o Brand Partnerships
- o Selling Products or Services
- o Coaching or Consulting
- o Creating Digital Products (e.g., courses, ebooks)

- Mastering the X Algorithm: Your Key to Success and Growth
- Stay Ahead of the Curve: Adapting to Changes and Updates

INTRODUCTION

Forget "going viral" fairy tales. Remember those perfect online lives? Yeah, fake news. The real game has hidden rules, and the boss is called Algorithm. I used to be a clueless player, posting like crazy to crickets. Then, I hacked the system. Not magic, just hard work and a bit of rebellion.

This ain't your boring guide. No robot talk or dry numbers. This is a secret manual, shared between creators like whispers in the dark. We're getting down and dirty with the Algorithm, understanding its tricks and hidden desires. Remember that time I accidentally banished myself to the online shadow realm? We'll laugh about that one later.

The truth is, mastering the Algorithm isn't about bowing down. It's about knowing the rules, then dancing around them like a mischievous fairy. It's turning your passion into a pixelated circus, where you're the star, the ringmaster, and the popcorn vendor all at once. It's building a fan club so passionate, so wild, that the Algorithm itself throws its hands up and says, "What in the world is happening over there?!"

So, brave creators, are you ready to ditch the hamster wheel and become the Algorithm's worst nightmare? This ain't for the faint of heart. We'll sweat, we'll rant, and we'll celebrate like rockstars when our followers blast off like rockets. This is your invitation to break free and rewrite the rules. Up for it? Let's go!

P.S. Next stop: dissecting the X Algorithm like a science experiment. Get ready to be amazed (and maybe a little scared) by its secrets.

CHAPTER 1:

DECODING THE ALGORITHM: CRACKING THE CODE TO CONTENT KINGDOM

Remember the thrill of cracking a childhood secret code? That triumphant "Got it!" moment when hidden words leap into focus? Mastering the X Algorithm is like that, but instead of whispered playground riddles, we're deciphering the code to online fame and fortune (or at least a following that makes your grandma do a jig of pride).

But hold on, ditch the "get rich quick" schemes and shady "growth hacks." Those are as real as a tap-dancing unicorn on Mars. Building a loyal following takes sweat, time, and understanding how the Algorithm ticks like a curious clockwork bird.

Think of the X Algorithm as the gatekeeper to Content Kingdom. It decides who gets seen, who gets heard, and who gets lost in the dreaded "digital dungeon" of obscurity. So, how do we win its favor? By learning its language, its preferences, and its occasional bouts of algorithmic weirdness.

Here's your decoder ring for those key factors that influence the Algorithm's decisions:

1. Content is King (or Queen, or Rockstar):

This ain't no place for fluff, my friend. We're talking engaging posts, informative articles, videos that make you snort milk out your nose – content that resonates with your audience like a perfectly tuned guitar in their soul. Ditch the boring and focus on creating stuff that rocks their world. Think captivating short stories, insightful tutorials, hilarious memes that capture the zeitgeist – content that makes them say, "Whoa, where did this awesomeness come from?"

Example: Sarah, a baker, used to post dry recipe descriptions. When she started sharing playful baking adventures, showcasing her mishaps and successes, her engagement skyrocketed. People connected with her authenticity and humor, her audience became her baking cheerleaders.

2. Know Your Tribe:

Who are you whispering your secrets to? What makes them tick, what keeps them up at night, what's their spirit animal (don't judge, everyone has one)? The more you understand your target audience, the better you can tailor your content to their deepest desires, like a tailor crafting a magical cloak of engagement. Think about their interests, their challenges, their online hangouts. Are they fitness enthusiasts on Instagram? Budding entrepreneurs on LinkedIn? Cat lovers on TikTok?

Example: Mark, a fitness blogger, used to post generic workout routines. When he started focusing on specific challenges faced by his audience (home workouts for busy parents, beginner-friendly exercises) and sharing their progress stories, his following surged. He spoke their language, understood their pain points, and became their go-to fitness guru.

3. Consistency is Your Compass:

The Algorithm loves a reliable friend. Show up like clockwork, post like a well-oiled machine, and treat your audience like they matter (because they do!). Building a loyal following takes time, so be patient and keep creating awesome stuff. Consistency is your compass, guiding you through the content wilderness. Think regular schedules, themed content days, engaging stories spread across posts.

Example: Emily, a travel blogger, used to post sporadically. When she started posting weekly travel tips on Mondays, inspiring photo stories on Wednesdays, and behind-the-scenes adventures on Fridays, her audience knew where to find her and eagerly awaited her next travel fix.

Remember, this is just the beginning of your journey. Stay tuned for Chapter 2, where we'll delve deeper into understanding your audience and creating content that truly connects. And keep an eye out for the bonus section in this chapter, where I'll share some real-life stories of how I used these tips to crack the X Algorithm and build a thriving online community.

Now go forth and conquer, content warrior! The online kingdom awaits!

4. Engagement is the Golden Ticket: Likes, comments, shares – these are the shiny coins of the Algorithm's realm. The more interaction your content gets, the brighter it shines in the digital sky. So, encourage discussion, ask questions like a curious explorer, and respond to your audience like you're having a real conversation (because you are!).

5. Hashtags are Your Secret Weapon: Think of hashtags as signposts leading people to your content goldmine. Use relevant hashtags that your audience is searching for, but don't go overboard with the #spam. Quality over quantity, remember? A well-chosen hashtag is like a treasure map leading people to your content oasis.

6. Timing is Everything: There's a magic hour for posting, a sweet spot when your audience is most active and ready to engage. Experiment with different times like a time-traveling alchemist, see what works best for you. Bonus points for scheduling your posts for peak times so you can be off living your best life while your content does the work.

7. **Don't Be Afraid to Experiment**: The Algorithm loves a little surprise. Try different formats, test out new ideas like a mad scientist in a content laboratory. The more you experiment, the more you'll learn what resonates with your audience and what gets lost in the digital void.

Remember, there's no magic potion for mastering the X Algorithm. It's a living, breathing beast (or at least a very complicated computer program), and its preferences can shift like the desert sands. But by understanding these key points and staying true to your voice and passion, you'll be well on your way to building a loyal following and carving your own corner of the online kingdom.

Now, go forth and conquer, content warrior! And remember, Chapter 2 awaits, ready to guide you on your journey to understanding your audience and creating content that truly connects. Keep an eye out for the bonus section at the end of this chapter, where I'll share some real-life stories of how I used these tips to crack the X Algorithm and build a thriving online community. Stay tuned!

P.S. Feeling overwhelmed? Remember, this is a journey, not a race. Take your time, have fun, and enjoy the process of building something amazing. The online kingdom awaits!

CHAPTER 2:

AUDIENCE ALCHEMY: TRANSFORMING STRANGERS INTO SUPERFANS

Remember the awkward phase of school dances? Staring across the gym at potential friends, unsure how to bridge the gap? Building an online audience can feel eerily similar – a room full of strangers on screens, waiting to be charmed into superfans. But fear not, content warriors! Chapter 2 is your secret decoder ring to audience alchemy, transforming those digital strangers into your cheering squad.

First, ditch the "spray and pray" approach. Bombarding the internet with random posts is like throwing spaghetti at the wall hoping some sticks. We need precision, my friends. To truly connect, we must understand our audience, their hopes, dreams, and deepest desires (okay, maybe not *that* deep, but you get the picture).

Think of it like a treasure hunt:

1. **Unmasking the Mystery**: Who are these digital voyagers you seek? Dive into their demographics, their online hangouts, the hashtags they chase. Are they bookworms on Reddit, aspiring artists on Instagram, or dog lovers on TikTok? Knowing their habitat is half the battle.

2. **Mapping the Motivations**: What makes their hearts tick? What challenges do they face? What sparks joy in their digital souls? Think about their goals, their fears, their deepest longings. Are they seeking career advice, artistic inspiration, or simply a laugh to break up the day? Understanding their needs is the key to crafting content that resonates.

3. **Building the Bridge**: Now, we build the bridge between your awesome content and their eager eyes. Speak their language, not some highfalutin' dictionary drivel. Use humor they understand, references they get, stories that mirror their lives. Think relatable anecdotes, engaging questions, and a dash of vulnerability to show you're human too.

Remember:

- Be a conversation starter, not a monologue machine. Encourage interaction, respond to comments, foster a sense of community.

- Show, don't tell. Paint vivid pictures with your words, showcase your expertise through examples, and let your passion shine through.

- Authenticity is your secret weapon. Be yourself, quirks and all. People connect with genuineness, not carefully curated personas.

Examples:

- When I started building on X, I tried going solo, no friends, no community and eventually it became boring and very stressful. Why? I tried to learn everything on my own. Solo building on X is not advisable get friends and mentor. This will be discussed in the later chapter of our book.

- David, a tech blogger, used to explain complex concepts in jargon. When he started using humor and everyday analogies, his followers soared. They laughed, learned, and crowned him their tech guru.

Building a loyal audience takes time and effort, but the rewards are sweeter than any online trophy. You'll create a community, find your voice, and maybe even make a living doing what you love. So, go forth, content alchemists! Transmute those strangers into superfans, build your online kingdom, and remember, Chapter 3 awaits, where we'll explore the art of captivating content creation – the fuel that fires the engine of audience engagement.

P.S. Feeling stuck? Don't despair! Experiment, try new things, and track what resonates. Your audience is a living, breathing entity, and your content should evolve with them. The journey is half the fun, so enjoy the ride, content warrior!

CHAPTER 3:

CONTENT CRAFT: FORGING THE GOLDEN HAMMERS OF ENGAGEMENT

Remember those childhood sandcastles? Pile after pile of wet sand, a bucket and a dream, hoping to sculpt something magical. Building captivating content can feel a bit like that – molding words into engaging nuggets that captivate your audience and make them click "follow" faster than a hummingbird on sugar. But fear not, content warriors! Chapter 3 is your secret blueprint for crafting the golden hammers of engagement, ready to sculpt online empires.

First, ditch the dry lectures and recycled blog posts. We're not building sandcastles in a hurricane here. We need variety, my friends, like a box of vibrant crayons waiting to paint your digital canvas. Think:

- Storytelling Sprouts: Weave narratives that pull your audience in like riptides. Share personal anecdotes, relatable struggles, and triumphs that feel like whispered secrets between friends. Make them laugh, cry, and scream "Yasss Queen!" (or King, or whatever royalty rocks your boat).

- Question Quakes: Throw out thought grenades that detonate discussions. Ask daring questions, spark debates, and encourage healthy (but lively!) back-and-forth. Remember, controversy can be your friend, just keep it respectful and avoid stepping on toes (unless it's the metaphorical toes of negativity, then stomp away!).

- Visual Volcanoes: Don't just tell, show! Images, videos, infographics – unleash the visual fireworks. Break up text with eye-catching visuals that complement your words and make your content a feast for the senses. Remember, a picture is worth a thousand likes, so paint a masterpiece!

- Humor Hummingbirds: Inject your content with a healthy dose of laughter. Witty one-liners, relatable memes, playful banter – let your personality shine through. Remember, people connect with authenticity and humor is the universal language of good vibes.

Examples:

- Based on study and experience, your content travel far when there is a photo or video attach to it. Images says thousands of words at the same time. Images or video add more content to your content, it gives your content a clearer definition.

The story telling should be in-line with your content. For example if you are digital marketer trying to build, your story telling should be about how you close your first sale, how your friends and family member did not believe you, how your client accuse you of been a scammer, basically your struggle and setback experience and it must be accompanied with how you overcame it.

Remember, content creation is a marathon, not a sprint. Experiment, find your voice, and don't be afraid to mess up. Your audience appreciates the journey as much as the destination. So, go forth, content crafters! Forge your golden hammers of engagement, sculpt your online kingdom, and remember, Chapter 4 awaits, where we'll explore the intricate dance of paid promotion and influencer collaborations – the secret sauce that can rocket your content to the top of the algorithm's food chain.

P.S. Feeling stuck? Don't despair! Analyze what resonates with your audience, track engagement metrics, and adapt your content like a chameleon on a rainbow. The journey is half the fun, so grab your metaphorical bucket and shovel, and let's build something phenomenal!

CHAPTER 4

ENGAGEMENT STRATEGIES: KEEPING YOUR AUDIENCE HOOKED

Welcome to the realm where engagement isn't just a metric; it's a dynamic dance between you and your audience. As we dive into the strategies that will transform casual onlookers into devoted followers, be prepared for a journey that transcends the mundane and taps into the extraordinary.

Section 1: The Power of a Compelling Story

In the grand tapestry of engagement, stories are the golden threads that weave connections. Picture this: You're not just sharing content; you're inviting your audience into a narrative where they play a vital role. From personal anecdotes to relatable tales, learn how to captivate hearts and minds with the ancient art of storytelling.

Section 2: The Art of the Unexpected

Ever felt the exhilaration of a plot twist in your favorite movie? Now, imagine injecting that thrill into your content. Discover the secret sauce of unpredictability and how it keeps your audience on the edge of their virtual seats. It's time to become the director of your audience's attention.

Section 3: Conversations, Not Monologues

Engagement is a two-way street, and monologues belong in history books. Explore the strategies of fostering genuine conversations with your audience. From thought-provoking questions to interactive polls, we'll redefine engagement as a dialogue where every voice matters.

Section 4: The Psychology of Engagement

Uncover the psychological triggers that transform passive scrolling into active participation. From the allure of exclusivity to the impact of social proof, we'll delve into the intricate workings of the human mind and how you can leverage these insights to create an engagement masterpiece.

Section 5: The Element of Surprise

Prepare to be the magician of the digital realm. Learn how to sprinkle surprise and delight into your content strategy, ensuring your audience never knows what gem awaits them. It's not just about breaking patterns; it's about creating moments that linger in the memory.

Section 6: From Engagement to Advocacy

In this final stretch, we'll navigate the terrain where engagement transforms into advocacy. It's not just about likes and comments; it's about having an army of ambassadors who champion your cause. Discover the strategies that turn casual followers into die-hard supporters.

As we traverse through these pages, remember: Engagement is not a formula but an evolving symphony. Each strategy is a note, and you, my friend, are the virtuoso conductor. Are you ready to orchestrate an engagement masterpiece that echoes in the hearts of your audience?

Engagement Engine: Keeping Your Audience Hooked Like a Cosmic Cliffhanger

Remember that exhilarating childhood moment when you finished a thrilling book, heart pounding, desperate to know what happens next? Building audience engagement can feel eerily similar – crafting content that keeps them scrolling, commenting, and begging for more like a cosmic cliffhanger. But fear not, content weavers! Chapter 4 is your secret decoder ring to the engagement engine, turning passive viewers into rabid fans who hang on your every word (or pixel).

Ditch the Monologue Machine: Forget one-way streets and dusty museums. Think of your content as a vibrant carnival, a bustling bazaar of interaction, where conversations crackle like fireworks and ideas dance like disco balls. We need two-way conversations, my friends, a never-ending loop of give and take that keeps your audience coming back for seconds, thirds, and the entire buffet of your awesomeness.

Throw Thought Grenades: Spark discussions that detonate like social media fireworks. Ask daring questions that ignite debates, the kind that have people tapping "agree" or "disagree" with the fervor of Olympic fencers. Remember, controversy can be your friend, as long as it's respectful and sparks healthy discourse, not digital dumpster fires.

Unleash the Poll Playground: Let your audience be the puppeteers! Design interactive polls, quizzes, and surveys that tap into their opinions and desires. Think trending topics, relatable dilemmas, or playful personality quizzes – give them a chance to play director in the content coliseum. Who's the morning person here? Who struggles with procrastination like a boss? Who secretly loves pineapple on pizza? Uncover the gems of audience data and tailor your content accordingly.

Foster the Comment Cosmos: Transform your comment section into a digital campfire, where conversations crackle with humor, insights, and shared experiences. Respond to comments with the warmth of a friendly barista, answer questions with the wit of a seasoned storyteller, and engage with your audience like they're fellow adventurers on your creative journey. Remember, acknowledging their presence and responding fosters a sense of community that keeps them coming back for the digital warmth.

Embrace the Live Launchpad: Channel the ephemeral magic of live content. Host live Q&A sessions, behind-the-scenes glimpses, or interactive workshops. Think impromptu challenges, real-time reactions, and a dose of unfiltered authenticity – give your audience a front-row seat to the rollercoaster of your creative process. Let them see the messy gears that turn your content machine, the stumbles and triumphs that make your journey unique.

Build the Community Compass: Forget just a following, cultivate a tribe. Create dedicated groups, forums, or online hangouts where your audience can connect, share, and support each other. Think shared goals, collaborative projects, and a sense of belonging – transform viewers into a vibrant community that thrives beyond your individual content. Remember, a strong community is like a self-perpetuating engine, where engagement fuels itself and your content prospers.

Remember These Golden Nuggets:

- Consistency is your fuel: Show up like a clockwork content machine, my friends. Regular engagement is the oxygen that keeps your audience alive, so respond promptly, keep the conversation flowing, and don't leave them gasping for air between content drops.

- Variety is the spice of life: Keep things fresh, content warriors! Experiment with formats, platforms, and engagement tactics like a chef trying out new flavor combinations. Think unexpected collaborations, guest appearances, or even switching up your posting schedule – predictability is the enemy of excitement.

- Authenticity is your secret weapon: Be yourself, quirks and all. People connect with genuineness, not carefully curated personas. Let your personality shine through, even if it's a bit messy and unscripted. Remember, realness resonates, and your audience will appreciate the human behind the content.

So, go forth, content weavers! Spin the gears of your engagement engine, keep your audience hooked like a cosmic cliffhanger, and remember, Chapter 5 awaits, where we'll explore the art of monetizing your hustle and turning your passion into profit – the ultimate reward for every successful content

CHAPTER 5:

CONQUERING THE X. MAZE: MASTERING THE ALGORITHM AND BUILDING YOUR BRAND

Remember that childhood thrill of navigating a complex maze, twists and turns keeping you on your toes, but ultimately leading to triumph? Building your brand on X. can feel eerily similar – a labyrinth of algorithms, trends, and audience preferences, with the ultimate prize being a loyal following and a thriving online presence. But fear not, brand-builders! Chapter 5 is your secret decoder ring to the X. maze, guiding you through the intricacies and emerging as a brand that shines brighter than any dead end.

First, ditch the "scatter and hope" approach. Throwing content into the X. void like lost marbles is a recipe for frustration. We need precision, my friends, a deep understanding of X.'s unique ecosystem and your audience's digital heartbeat. Think:

1. **Know Your Crowd on X.**: Who are you whispering your brand secrets to? Delve into your audience's demographics, their X. haunts, their online quirks. Are they

early morning scrollers, lunchtime lurkers, or late-night laugh seekers? Understanding their rhythm within X.'s specific algorithms is the first step to hitting the right notes.

2. **Decode the X. Algorithm**: X.'s algorithm is the gatekeeper of this digital kingdom. Learn its language, brand warriors! Track peak times, analyze engagement data, understand when your audience is most receptive to your brand message. Think trending topics, hashtags that resonate, and even X.-specific features – ride the algorithm's wave, don't fight its current.

3. **Content is Your Compass**: Remember, X. is a content jungle. Carve your path with engaging, high-quality content that speaks to your audience's needs and desires. Think:

- Video Voyages: X. thrives on visuals, so unleash the power of captivating videos! Showcase your brand's personality, tell your story, and offer value through tutorials, product demos, or behind-the-scenes glimpses.

- Livestreaming Landmarks: X. is all about real-time connection. Host live Q&A sessions, product launches, or interactive events. Build a sense of community, answer questions in real-time, and let your audience be part of your brand journey.

- Collaboration Collages: X. is a world of collaboration. Partner with other brands, influencers, or creators in your niche. Cross-promote, co-create content, and tap into each other's audiences – think win-win synergies that expand your reach and brand awareness.

4. **Consistency is Your Currency**: Show up like a clockwork brand-builder, my friends. Regular content drops keep your audience engaged and prevent them from wandering to other brands in the X. maze. Remember, consistency is key to building trust and loyalty.

5. **Analyze and Adapt**: Like a seasoned explorer, be nimble and adaptable. Track your results with eagle eyes. Analyze clicks, views, engagement – find what makes your brand resonate and what leaves it lost in the X. wilderness. Remember, data is your compass, not a rigid map.

Examples:

- Sarah, the fitness coach, used to post sporadically on X. When she started creating consistent workout routines, live X.-exclusive tutorials, and interactive challenges, her audience soared. She carved a clear path through the X. maze and became a go-to brand for fitness enthusiasts on the platform.

- David, the tech blogger, used to rely on generic content. When he started collaborating with other tech creators on X., hosting live product reviews, and showcasing his expertise through in-depth X.-specific tutorials, his brand exploded. He partnered with the algorithm and other brands to conquer the X. maze and build a loyal following.

Remember:

- **Authenticity is Your Golden Thread**: Be yourself, brand warriors! Let your unique voice and personality shine through. People connect with genuineness, not carefully curated personas.

- **Engagement is Your Fuel**: Don't just broadcast, interact! Respond to comments, answer questions, and foster a sense of community around your brand. Remember, engagement is the bridge that connects you to your audience.

- **Data is Your Lighthouse**: Analyze your results, track trends, and adapt your strategy like a seasoned navigator. X. is a constantly evolving landscape, so stay informed and adjust your sails accordingly.

So, go forth, brand-builders! Conquer the X. maze, make your brand the brightest beacon in the digital jungle, and remember, Chapter 6 awaits, where we'll explore the art of staying resilient and navigating the inevitable challenges of the online journey – the final step in building a brand that stands tall amidst the twists and turns of X.'s ever-changing landscape.

P.S. Feeling lost in the X. maze? Don't despair! Analyze your audience's activity patterns, track platform trends, and

CHAPTER 6:

HASHTAG HACKS: CRACKING THE CODE TO CONTENT CONQUEST

Remember that childhood treasure hunt, deciphering cryptic clues and unearthing buried riches? Mastering the art of hashtags on X. can feel eerily similar – wielding these tiny symbols like shovels, digging deep into the platform's hidden potential and unearthing a buried pot of followers, engagement, and maybe even a viral unicorn or two. But fear not, hashtag heroes! Chapter 6 is your secret treasure map, guiding you through the labyrinthine world of hashtags and unleashing the true power of these digital pickaxes.

First, ditch the shotgun approach. Spraying random hashtags like confetti at a birthday party is a recipe for online oblivion. We need precision, my friends, a laser focus on relevant, trending, and audience-specific hashtags that act like golden gates to new realms of eyeballs and engagement. Think:

> ➢ Know Your Crowd: Who are you whispering your secret hashtags to? Delve into your audience's online language, the hashtags they frequent, the communities they engage with. Are they #fitnessfreaks, #foodiesofinstagram, or #mememastersoftiktok? Speaking their hashtag language is the first step to unlocking the treasure chest of their attention.

> Trendify Your Treasure Hunt: Don't get stuck digging in dusty corners. Research trending hashtags on X., seasonal spikes, and niche-specific conversations. Think holidays, current events, or even platform challenges – ride the hashtag wave, don't just watch it crash from the shore.

> Variety is the Spice of Discovery: Don't stick to the same old tired hashtags like a broken compass. Experiment with different combinations, test out niche and trending terms, and even create your own branded hashtags to build a loyal tribe. Remember, variety keeps the treasure hunt exciting, both for you and your audience.

> Quantity Can Be Quality: It's not just about finding the right hashtag, it's about finding the right amount. Think strategic sprinkling, not hashtag avalanche. Research optimal hashtag numbers for each platform, avoid keyword stuffing, and prioritize relevance over quantity.

Remember:

• Specificity is Your Shovel: Forget generic hashtags like #amazing or #loveit. Go deeper, my friends! Use targeted hashtags that speak directly to your content and your audience's interests. Think #yogateachertraining or #veganbakingchallenge – the more specific, the more likely you are to unearth buried treasure.

• Data is Your Treasure Map: Track your hashtag performance like a seasoned cartographer. Analyze which ones generate engagement, conversions, or even a viral sparkle. Ditch the duds, double down on the diamonds, and keep refining your hashtag strategy like a master prospector.

- Engagement is Your Golden Nugget: Hashtags are just the key, not the treasure itself. Engage with other users who use your hashtags, participate in relevant conversations, and build genuine connections. Remember, it's not just about reaching, it's about belonging.

Examples:

- Sarah, the fitness coach, used to slap generic #fitness hashtags on her posts. When she started researching trending workout challenges, incorporating niche terms like #yogaflowfriday, and even creating her own #strongmamacommunity hashtag, her engagement skyrocketed. She unearthed a hidden tribe of passionate yogis and built a thriving online community.

- David, the tech blogger, used to rely on broad #techie hashtags. When he started incorporating trending tech news hashtags, focusing on specific product reviews with targeted terms like #unboxingiphone14, and even launching a branded #asktechdavid hashtag for audience Q&A

sessions, his reach exploded. He navigated the X. maze with laser-focused hashtags and created a loyal following of tech enthusiasts.

So, go forth, hashtag heroes! Crack the code to content conquest, wield your hashtags like shimmering shovels, and unearth the buried riches of engagement, followers, and maybe even a bit of viral magic. Remember, Chapter 6 is just the beginning of your hashtag adventure. With every trend you ride, every niche you explore, you build not just a hashtag portfolio, but a map to online success that shines brighter than any buried treasure. Now go forth, and dig deep!

P.S. Feeling lost in the hashtag jungle? Don't despair! Analyze your platform's trending topics, research competitor hashtags, and experiment with different combinations. Remember, even the most seasoned treasure hunters need a little trial and error to strike gold. Keep digging, keep experimenting, and the online riches await!

CHAPTER 7:

THE SYNERGY EFFECT: BUILDING WITH FRIENDS AND FELLOW CREATORS

Remember that childhood magic of two best friends, fingers intertwined, facing down the playground bully, not as isolated peas, but as an unstoppable force of united giggles and muddy fist bumps? Building an online presence can feel eerily similar – harnessing the "synergy effect," where one plus one doesn't just equal two, it explodes into a supernova of reach, engagement, and creative fire. But fear not, collaboration warriors! Chapter 7 is your secret decoder ring to this symbiotic universe, guiding you to forge alliances and build empires that leave solo ventures in the dust.

Unleash the Co-Creation Kraken:

Imagine brainstorming with a fellow foodie friend, your kitchens transformed into culinary battlegrounds as you dream up the most outrageous vegan sushi burrito the world has ever seen. Or picture joining forces with a fashion stylist bestie, Instagram ablaze with the fire of a #MismatchedMondays challenge, every outfit a daring mix of polka dots and plaid. This, my friends, is the beauty of co-creation:

- Cross-pollinate your content: Fuse your skills, your audiences, your passions! Think cooking tutorials where your friend dissects the science of baking while you add the artistic flourishes. Imagine fashion challenges where you tackle thrift store finds while your bestie conjures runway-worthy looks from forgotten garments. Remember, combined audiences mean double the exposure, double the fun, and double the creative chaos.

- Challenge the algorithm together: Forget solo dance-offs with the TikTok algorithm. Think epic team-up flash mobs, your combined moves so electrifying they melt the digital walls and set the platform ablaze. Imagine collaborative photo challenges where you document a day in the life of your city, each angle revealing a different facet of urban vibrancy. Remember, joint contests, interactive campaigns, and shared creativity are kryptonite to the algorithm's resistance.

- Guest appearances and takeovers: Step aside, boring routines! Imagine swapping platforms with your friend, your X. stories bursting with the infectious laughter of a guest takeover. Picture hosting a Q&A session on their Youtube channel, your voices weaving a tapestry of expert advice and hilarious anecdotes. Remember, fresh voices, cross-promotional magic, and the element of surprise – collaboration keeps the content cauldron bubbling with innovation.

EMBRACE THE POWER OF PARTNERSHIPS:

Remember that playground bully cowering before the unified front of you and your best friend? Now picture channeling that synergy to conquer the online landscape. Brand deals, sponsorships, influencer groups – these are your allies, your co-pilots on the rocket ship to content superstardom:

- Brand deals, sponsorships, and influencer groups: Don't shy away from mutually beneficial partnerships with brands or fellow creators. Imagine collaborating with a local yoga studio to host mindfulness workshops, your expertise blended with their tranquil ambiance. Picture joining an influencer group focused on sustainable living, your content amplified by a chorus of like-minded voices. Remember, partnerships open doors you never knew existed, offering resources, reach, and a collective punch that resonates far beyond solo efforts.

- Leverage the influencer landscape: Think of an online jungle teeming with content creators, ripe for exploration and collaboration. Imagine diving into Facebook groups dedicated to your niche, sharing knowledge, offering support, and forming bonds that transcend the screen. Picture attending industry events, conferences, or workshops, your network blossoming with every handshake and shared brainstorm. Remember, the influencer landscape is a fertile ground for forging partnerships, learning from each other, and propelling each other's success.

FIND YOUR TRIBE, SEEK YOUR SYNERGY:

Remember that playground sandbox, a microcosm of childhood friendships forged through shared giggles and mud pies? Online communities are your new sandboxes, waiting to be filled with the laughter and creativity of fellow creators:

- Active participation in online communities: Dive into Discord servers buzzing with passionate discussions, Facebook groups bursting with shared tips, and X.-specific forums dedicated to your content niche. Imagine offering guidance, participating in debates, and building genuine connections with like-minded souls. Remember, online communities are not just echo chambers, but fertile ground for finding your tribe, learning from each other, and igniting collaborative sparks.

- Networking events and conferences: Step away from the screen and into the real world! Imagine attending industry events, workshops, or online conferences, your mind expanding with every shared insight and your network growing with every handshake. Picture pitching your collaborative ideas to potential partners, your voices a symphony of possibilities. Remember, the human connection forged in real-world interactions can transcend the digital divide, solidifying partnerships and igniting the fires of shared ambition.

Remember:

- Choose wisely, my friends: Not all collaborations are created equal. Seek partners who share your values, complement your content, and bring a unique perspective to the table. Remember, a harmonious blend of skills and personalities is key to a successful team-up.

CHAPTER 8:

PAID PROMOTION: NAVIGATING THE MINEFIELD TO MAXIMIZE YOUR REACH

Remember that childhood thrill of winning a free raffle ticket, a golden key unlocking a wonderland of candy and prizes? Paid promotion on platforms like X. can feel eerily similar – a strategic investment with the potential to catapult your content from a whisper in the void to a roaring symphony that captures the platform's attention. But fear not, promotional pioneers! Chapter 8 is your treasure map through the sometimes-treacherous terrain of paid ads, guiding you to unlock the riches of increased reach, engagement, and ultimate content domination.

Before You Dig for Digital Gold:

Before you unleash your inner tycoon and start throwing virtual coins at the algorithm, take a deep breath and ponder these pearls of wisdom:

- Know your goals, oh savvy spender: Are you hunting for new followers, driving traffic to your website, or sparking engagement on specific content? Identifying your objectives is like charting your course – it ensures your ad dollars don't get lost in the digital wilderness.

- Target your audience with laser precision: Don't cast your promotional net into the vast ocean of X. users. Craft detailed audience personas, considering demographics, interests, and online behavior. Remember, a targeted ad is a bullseye, not a blindfolded dart throw.

- Content is still king, even in the paid arena: Don't expect a sprinkle of ad dust to transform mediocre content into viral gold. Invest in high-quality, engaging content that resonates with your target audience. Remember, paid promotion amplifies your message, not replaces it.

Choose Your Weapon Wisely:

X. offers a treasure trove of promotional tools, each with its unique strengths and quirks. Choose wisely, my friends, for your weapon determines your battlefield dominance:

- Sponsored Posts: Think of these as VIP passes to the X. feed. Pay to have your content showcased prominently, directly in front of your target audience's eyes. Remember, sponsored posts are like billboards on the digital highway – attention-grabbing and impactful.

- Targeted Ads: These are the ninja stars of promotion, silently flitting through X. feeds, landing with precision on the interests of your chosen audience. Experiment with different formats, from video ads to carousel images, and track their effectiveness like a seasoned hunter.

- Collaborations and Influencer Marketing: Partner with established creators in your niche, leveraging their audiences and credibility to reach new heights. Think co-created sponsored content or influencer shoutouts – it's like borrowing someone else's megaphone to amplify your message.

Remember:

- Track, analyze, and adapt, like a data-driven warrior: Don't just throw money at the algorithm and hope for the best! Monitor your campaign performance, analyze engagement metrics, and tweak your approach based on the data. Remember, flexibility is key in the ever-changing landscape of paid promotion.

- Budget wisely, friends, for resources are finite: Set realistic spending limits and stick to them. Remember, paid promotion is a marathon, not a sprint, and sustainable success requires strategic resource allocation.

- Transparency is your shield: Be upfront with your audience about sponsored content. Building trust is key to maintaining your online reputation, even in the realm of paid promotion.

Examples:

- Sarah, the fitness coach, used targeted ads to promote her new online yoga course. By focusing on yoga enthusiasts in her local area, she saw a significant increase in course enrollments and local workshop attendance.

- David, the tech blogger, collaborated with a popular phone case brand on a sponsored video review. The combined reach of both audiences resulted in a viral hit, boosting brand awareness for both David and the phone case company.

So, go forth, promotional pioneers! Navigate the paid ad landscape with strategic precision, wield your chosen weapons with purpose, and remember, Chapter 8 is just the beginning of your journey to content mastery. With every targeted campaign, every analyzed metric, you build not just an online empire, but a legacy of innovation and reach that shines brighter than any paid gem. Now go forth, and claim your digital gold!

P.S. Feeling lost in the ad labyrinth? Don't despair! Research successful promotional campaigns in your niche, consult X. advertising guides, and experiment with different ad formats. Remember, even the most seasoned gold miners need a little trial and error to strike it rich. Keep digging, keep experimenting, and the digital riches await!

CHAPTER 9:

IDENTIFYING OPPORTUNITIES: ALIGNING YOUR PASSION WITH PROFIT

Remember that childhood lemonade stand, a cardboard banner and sunshine-squeezed sweetness, transforming backyard pennies into sugary riches? Monetizing your X. hustle can feel eerily similar – finding the sweet spot where your passions ignite, your content resonates, and the digital coins start clinking happily in your online piggy bank. But fear not, monetization maestros! Chapter 9 is your secret recipe for turning lemons into gold, guiding you to identify opportunities that align your creative fire with financial fulfilment.

Know thyself, oh content creator:

Before you dive headfirst into the monetization pool, take a moment for introspection. Ask yourself:

- What sets my soul on fire? What content do you create with infectious enthusiasm? What topics make your eyes sparkle and your fingers fly across the keyboard? Remember, genuine passion is the secret ingredient in any successful monetization strategy.

- What value do I offer? How does your content improve, educate, or entertain your audience? What unique skills or knowledge do you bring to the X. table? Remember, identifying your value proposition is like finding the perfect lemon – tart enough to pique interest, but juicy enough to quench a need.

- Who are my digital neighbors? Analyze your audience demographics, their online habits, and their spending patterns. Understanding your tribe's desires and resources is like mapping the path to the lemonade stand with the longest line.

The Monetization Menu:

Now that you've squeezed the juiciest bits of self-awareness, it's time to explore the diverse flavors of monetization:

- Direct Sales: Think e-books, online courses, downloadable printables, or even custom artwork or crafts. If your content inspires action, offer tangible products they can't resist. Remember, direct sales are like putting a price tag on your expertise, a sweet reward for your content creation efforts.

- Brand Partnerships and Sponsored Content: Collaborate with brands whose values align with yours. Promote their products, create sponsored content, or even host exclusive events. Remember, brand partnerships are like adding a dash of brand magic to your lemonade stand, attracting new customers and expanding your reach.

- Affiliate Marketing: Recommend products or services relevant to your content and earn a commission for each purchase made through your unique affiliate link. Think of it as adding a "pay-per-sip" element to your online stand, rewarding yourself for every satisfied customer.

- Paid Memberships and Subscriptions: Offer exclusive content, early access to videos, or behind-the-scenes glimpses to your loyal fans. Remember, memberships are like VIP passes to your content kingdom, enticing dedicated audience members with an extra squeeze of value.

Remember:

- Authenticity is your secret ingredient: Don't sell out! Promote products and services you genuinely believe in, or your audience will taste the bitterness of inauthenticity. Remember, trust is the sugar that keeps your lemonade stand thriving.

- Content is still king, even in the monetization kingdom: Don't let the clinking of digital coins drown out your creative voice. Keep producing high-quality content that resonates with your audience, and the monetization opportunities will follow like thirsty customers on a hot day.

- Diversify your menu, cater to different tastes: Don't rely on just one monetization method. Experiment with different options, find what works best for your niche and audience, and create a well-rounded financial feast.

Examples:

- Sarah, the fitness coach, used her passion for yoga to create an online course on beginner poses. She also partnered with a local yoga apparel brand for sponsored content and offered exclusive discounts to her followers.

- David, the tech blogger, became an affiliate for a popular phone case company. He also launched a paid membership club offering early access to product reviews and in-depth tech tutorials.

So, go forth, monetization maestros! Squeeze the essence of your passions, stir in a dash of self-awareness, and brew a concoction of content and opportunity that leaves your audience refreshed and your digital piggy bank overflowing. Remember, Chapter 9 is just the beginning of your monetization journey. With every identified opportunity, every successful partnership, you build not just a profitable X. empire, but a legacy of passion and purpose that tastes sweeter than any homemade lemonade. Now go forth, and raise a toast to your online success!

P.S. Feeling lost in the monetization maze? Don't despair! Research successful creators in your niche, analyze their income streams, and experiment with different monetization options. Remember, even the most seasoned lemonade stand owners needed a few practice runs before mastering the art of the perfect pour. Keep experimenting, keep tweaking, and the sweet taste of success awaits!

CHAPTER 10:

BUILDING A BRAND: ESTABLISHING YOUR EXPERTISE

Remember that childhood hero, the one whose name echoed through the playground, a beacon of coolness and know-how? Building your brand on X. can feel eerily similar – carving your name in the digital sands, etching your expertise onto the platform's consciousness, and becoming the go-to guru in your niche. But fear not, branding architects! Chapter 10 is your blueprint to crafting a brand that resonates, a brand that whispers "expert" in every pixel and syllable.

Lay the Foundation: Know Yourself, Know Your Audience:

Before you raise the digital hammer and chisel, take a moment for architectural introspection:

- What makes your brand unique? What sets you apart from the crowd of content creators? Is it your quirky humor, your in-depth knowledge, or your infectious enthusiasm? Remember, a unique brand is like a house with a distinctive roofline – it stands out from the cookie-cutter monotony.

- Who are your digital neighbors? Analyze your audience demographics, their online habits, and their aspirations. Understanding their needs and desires is like laying the foundation on solid ground – it ensures your brand resonates and doesn't crumble in the face of shifting trends.

- What are your brand values? What principles do you stand for? What message do you want to communicate to the world? Remember, strong brand values are like load-bearing walls – they provide structure, support, and a sense of purpose to your online edifice.

Craft Your Story, Brick by Brick:

Now that the blueprint is clear, it's time to lay the storytelling bricks:

- Consistency is key: Show up like a reliable contractor, my friend! Regularly post content, maintain a consistent voice and aesthetic, and build trust with your audience through unwavering presence. Remember, consistency is the mortar that binds your brand together, brick by digital brick.

- Quality over quantity: Don't just churn out content like mass-produced bricks. Focus on creating high-quality, informative, or entertaining pieces that resonate with your audience and showcase your expertise. Remember, quality is the architectural flourish that elevates your brand from ordinary to extraordinary.

- Engage with your audience: Foster a community around your brand. Respond to comments, participate in discussions, and show your audience you're not just a digital statue. Remember, engagement is the open windows and doors that invite people into your brand's warm, welcoming interior.

Showcase Your Expertise, Polish the Facade:

Once the foundation is laid and the story woven, it's time to polish your brand's facade:

- Visual identity: Design a logo, choose a color palette, and curate visuals that reflect your brand's personality and values. Remember, your visual identity is the paint job that makes your brand stand out on the digital street.

- Content pillars: Identify the key themes and topics that define your brand's expertise. These are your content pillars, the sturdy support beams that hold up your online structure. Remember, focusing on specific themes attracts a targeted audience and reinforces your expert image.

- Collaborations and partnerships: Team up with other creators, brands, or influencers in your niche. Cross-promote content, co-host events, and tap into each other's audiences. Remember, strategic collaborations are like decorative arches that add depth and dimension to your brand's landscape.

Remember:

- Authenticity is your architect's license: Don't try to be someone you're not. Your audience can smell inauthenticity from a mile away. Be true to yourself, your values, and your voice, and your brand will resonate with genuine charm.

- Adapt and evolve, like a master builder: The digital landscape is constantly shifting. Stay informed about trends, experiment with new formats, and adapt your brand accordingly. Remember, flexibility is the scaffolding that allows you to adjust and grow with the changing tide.

- Patience is your trowel: Building a strong brand takes time and dedication. Don't get discouraged by slow progress. Keep laying those bricks, one by one, and eventually, your brand will rise like a magnificent testament to your expertise.

Examples:

- Sarah, the fitness coach, crafted a brand built around her passion for yoga and mindfulness. She consistently posted high-quality yoga tutorials, hosted live Q&A sessions, and collaborated with local wellness brands. Her dedication and authenticity cemented her position as the go-to yoga guru in her online community.

- David, the tech blogger, established himself as a tech expert through in-depth product reviews, insightful commentary on industry trends, and collaborations with tech companies. He built a strong brand with a loyal following of tech enthusiasts who valued his knowledge and trusted his opinions.

So, go forth, branding architects! Raise the digital hammer, lay the bricks of expertise, and craft a brand that resonates, a

CHAPTER 11:

CREATING ENGAGING CONTENT: FOSTERING A LOYAL FOLLOWING

Remember that childhood campfire, crackling flames casting dancing shadows, stories whispered and shared, laughter echoing through the night? Crafting engaging content on X. can feel eerily similar – igniting a digital fire of creativity, weaving tales that captivate, and fostering a loyal tribe of followers who gather around your virtual flames. But fear not, content conjurers! Chapter 11 is your secret recipe for concocting content that sparks, a guide to building a community that warms the coldest corners of the online world.

Know Your Audience, Stoke the Right Fire:

Before you toss the first metaphorical log onto the digital pyre, take a moment to understand your audience:

- What are their interests and passions? What topics make their eyes light up? What problems do they seek solutions to? Remember, your audience is the kindling – knowing their preferences ensures your content sparks the right kind of fire.

- What format resonates with them? Do they devour long-form articles, crave the bite-sized thrills of videos, or lose themselves in the interactive magic of live streams? Remember, format is the tinder – choose the one that ignites your audience's curiosity and keeps them coming back for more.

- What tone speaks to them? Do they respond to playful humor, insightful analysis, or heartfelt vulnerability? Remember, tone is the bellows – choose the one that fans the flames of engagement and keeps the conversation flowing.

Fuel the Fire with Variety and Quality:

Once you know your audience's kindling, it's time to stack the logs of content:

- Diversity is key: Don't get stuck in a rut of monotonous content. Experiment with different formats, explore new topics, and surprise your audience with unexpected twists. Remember, variety is the firewood – it keeps the fire burning bright and prevents boredom from extinguishing the flames.

- Quality is paramount: Don't just toss any old log onto the pyre. Strive for high-quality content that is informative, entertaining, or emotionally resonant. Remember, quality is the craftsmanship – it ensures your content burns long and leaves a lasting impression.

- Storytelling is your secret weapon: Weave narratives into your content, whether it's a personal anecdote, a case study, or a fictional adventure. Remember, stories are the emotional kindling – they draw your audience in, connect them to your message, and create a sense of shared experience.

Fan the Flames with Interaction and Community:

Content alone isn't enough to build a loyal tribe. Tend to the fire of community with these embers of engagement:

- Respond to comments and messages: Show your audience you care! Take the time to answer questions, address concerns, and acknowledge their feedback. Remember, responsiveness is the oxygen – it keeps the fire of conversation alive and thriving.

- Host live streams, Q&A sessions, and interactive events: Create opportunities for real-time interaction and connection. Give your audience a chance to participate, ask questions, and feel like part of something bigger. Remember, interactivity is the bellows – it fans the flames of community and fosters a sense of belonging.

- Encourage user-generated content: Let your audience become part of the storytelling. Invite them to share their experiences, photos, or creative interpretations of your content. Remember, user-generated content is the shared firewood – it adds warmth and authenticity to your digital campfire.

Remember:

- Authenticity is your magic spark: Don't try to be someone you're not. Your audience can smell inauthenticity from a mile away. Be true to yourself, your voice, and your passions, and your content will resonate with genuine warmth.

- Consistency is your fuel: Show up like a reliable storyteller, my friend! Regularly post new content, maintain a consistent schedule, and treat your audience with respect. Remember, consistency is the steady wood supply – it keeps the fire burning bright and prevents it from dying out.

- Adapt and evolve, like a master storyteller: The online landscape is constantly shifting. Stay informed about trends, experiment with new formats, and adapt your content accordingly. Remember, flexibility is the wind that carries your stories far and wide, reaching new audiences and igniting new flames.

Examples:

- Sarah, the fitness coach, used storytelling to weave her exercise routines into narratives of personal growth and empowerment. She hosted live Q&A sessions, encouraged user-generated workout videos, and fostered a community of supportive fitness enthusiasts around her virtual campfire.

- David, the tech blogger, created interactive quizzes and polls to engage his audience, hosted live product reviews with viewers' questions, and invited guest speakers to share their insights. He built a loyal following of tech-savvy individuals who gathered around his digital fire to learn, share, and connect.

So, go forth, content conjurers! Light the digital pyre

CHAPTER 12:

THE MASTERMIND APPROACH: FINDING A MENTOR AND BUILDING A SUPPORT SYSTEM

Remember that childhood quest for the sage old wizard, the one who held the secrets to success, a hidden mentor ready to unlock your hidden potential? Building your online presence on X. can feel eerily similar – a journey where guidance and support can illuminate the path and propel you towards mastery. But fear not, aspiring adventurers! Chapter 12 is your treasure map to finding the mentors and allies who will empower your journey, a testament to the power of the "mastermind approach."

Seeking Guidance: Identifying the Wise Ones:

Before you embark on your mentorship quest, cast your analytical eye:

- What are your areas of growth? Identify the skills, knowledge gaps, or strategic blind spots that hinder your progress. Remember, a targeted search for guidance yields a mentor who addresses your specific needs.

- Where do you seek wisdom? Explore online communities, industry events, or professional networks. Research established creators in your niche, analyze their content, and identify potential mentors whose expertise resonates with your aspirations. Remember, the mentor-to-be might be just a virtual handshake away.

- Approach with respect and clarity: When reaching out to potential mentors, be professional, specific, and express your genuine interest in learning from their experience. Remember, respect and clear communication lay the foundation for a fruitful mentorship relationship.

The Power of Mentorship: Unlocking Hidden Potential:

Once you've found your wise one, prepare to reap the rewards:

- Experience is the ultimate teacher: Learn from your mentor's successes and failures, gaining valuable insights that shortcut your own learning curve. Remember, a seasoned mentor's guidance can save you from years of trial and error.

- Feedback is the fuel for growth: Embrace your mentor's constructive criticism, using it as a springboard for improvement. Remember, honest feedback refines your skills and propels you closer to mastery.

- Motivation is a flickering flame: Let your mentor be the wind that keeps your creative fire burning bright. Seek encouragement, share your challenges, and find renewed inspiration in their unwavering support. Remember, a true mentor believes in your potential even when you doubt yourself.

Building Your Support Network: No One Climbs Alone:

Your mentor is your personal Everest guide, but the landscape of X. demands a broader support system:

- Mastermind groups: Assemble a tribe of like-minded creators, a forum for sharing ideas, offering peer feedback, and holding each other accountable. Remember, collective brainstorming ignites innovation, and shared struggles lighten the load.

- Accountability partners: Find a fellow X. adventurer, someone who will check in on your progress, celebrate your wins, and nudge you forward when you falter. Remember, a supportive partner keeps you on track and prevents you from losing momentum.

- Online communities: Dive into forums, Discord servers, or Facebook groups dedicated to your niche. Find your tribe, offer support in return, and learn from the collective wisdom of your peers. Remember, community is the fertile ground where inspiration, advice, and collaboration blossom.

Remember:

- Respect and reciprocity are the golden threads: Treat your mentors and support network with the same respect and dedication you expect in return. Remember, a healthy network thrives on mutual support and shared growth.

- Openness is the key to unlocking potential: Be vulnerable, share your challenges, and embrace feedback. Remember, closed minds limit your growth, while open hearts and minds unlock hidden potential.

- Lifelong learning is the ultimate quest: Never stop seeking guidance, support, and new perspectives. Remember, the journey to mastery is never-ending, and your network is your compass on the ever-evolving landscape of X.

Examples:

- Sarah, the fitness coach, found a mentor in a seasoned yoga instructor who provided invaluable feedback on her content and training techniques. She also joined a mastermind group of female fitness coaches, finding a supportive community to share ideas and hold each other accountable.

- David, the tech blogger, connected with a veteran tech journalist who offered sage advice on navigating the industry and building his online presence. He also participated in online forums, collaborating with fellow tech enthusiasts on content creation and industry analysis.

So, go forth, aspiring adventurers! Seek the wisdom of mentors, build a network of support, and remember, Chapter 12 is just the beginning of your mastermind journey. With every piece of advice received, every challenge overcome with your tribe, you climb not just the mountain of X. success, but the summit of your own creative potential. Now go forth, and claim your digital mastery!

P.S. Feeling lost in the mentorship maze? Don't despair! Research successful creators in your niche, analyze their mentors and networks, and don't be afraid to reach out for guidance. Remember, even the most accomplished adventurers needed a helping hand

CHAPTER 13:

MONETIZATION METHODS: TURNING YOUR PASSION INTO INCOME

Remember that childhood lemonade stand, a cardboard banner and sunshine-squeezed sweetness, transforming backyard pennies into sugary riches? Monetizing your X. hustle can feel eerily similar – finding the sweet spot where your passions ignite, your content resonates, and the digital coins start clinking happily in your online piggy bank. But fear not, monetization maestros! Chapter 13 is your secret recipe for turning lemons into gold, offering a diverse menu of methods to transform your passion into profit.

Affiliate Marketing: Be the Pied Piper of products!

- Partner with brands relevant to your niche and promote their products through sponsored content, affiliate links, or dedicated reviews.

- Earn a commission for every purchase made through your unique affiliate link, turning your audience's shopping sprees into your earning spree.

- Remember, transparency is key! Disclose your affiliate partnerships and only recommend products you genuinely believe in.

Brand Partnerships: Let your X. fame attract brand magic!

- Collaborate with established brands for sponsored content, product placements, or exclusive campaigns.

- Leverage the brand's reach and reputation to boost your own visibility and credibility.

- Remember, choose partners whose values align with yours, ensuring your content remains authentic and resonates with your audience.

Selling Products or Services: Unleash your inner entrepreneur!

- Design and sell physical products like merchandise, handmade crafts, or personalized creations inspired by your content.

- Offer digital products like e-books, online courses, downloadable templates, or exclusive printables showcasing your expertise.

- Remember, high-quality products and valuable services are key to customer satisfaction and repeat business.

Coaching or Consulting: Share your wisdom, watch wallets open!

- Offer one-on-one coaching or consulting services to clients seeking your expertise in your niche.

- Conduct online workshops, mastermind groups, or personalized training sessions based on your specific skills and knowledge.

- Remember, personalized attention and tangible results are essential for attracting and retaining coaching clients.

Creating Digital Products: Become a content king (or queen)!

- Develop in-depth online courses, comprehensive ebooks, or insightful video tutorials that provide valuable takeaways for your audience.

- Offer exclusive memberships or subscription services with early access to content, bonus materials, or behind-the-scenes glimpses.

- Remember, high-quality content, regular updates, and ongoing value delivery are crucial for retaining subscription-based customers.

Remember:

- Diversify your menu: Don't rely on just one monetization method. Experiment with different options, find what works best for your niche and audience, and create a well-rounded financial feast.

- Authenticity is your secret ingredient: Only promote products or services you genuinely believe in. Your audience can smell inauthenticity from a mile away, so keep your recommendations honest and ethical.

- Content is still king, even in the monetization kingdom: Don't let the clinking of digital coins drown out your creative voice. Keep producing high-quality content that resonates with your audience, and the monetization opportunities will follow like thirsty customers on a hot day.

Examples:

- Sarah, the fitness coach, combined affiliate marketing with her own e-book on yoga poses for beginners. She also offered personalized coaching sessions and partnered with a local sportswear brand for sponsored content and exclusive discounts for her followers.

- David, the tech blogger, created an in-depth online course on cybersecurity for beginners. He partnered with a tech security company for brand promotions and offered exclusive consulting services to small businesses.

So, go forth, monetization maestros! Squeeze the essence of your passions, stir in a dash of strategy, and brew a concoction of content and opportunity that leaves your audience refreshed and your X. piggy bank overflowing. Remember, Chapter 13 is just the beginning of your financial journey. With every new revenue stream, every satisfied customer, you build not just a profitable X. empire, but a legacy of passion and purpose that tastes sweeter than any homemade lemonade. Now go forth, and raise a toast to your online success!

P.S. Feeling lost in the monetization maze? Don't despair! Research successful creators in your niche, analyze their income streams, and experiment with different monetization options. Remember, even the most seasoned lemonade stand owners needed a few practice runs before mastering the art of the perfect pour. Keep experimenting, keep tweaking, and the sweet taste of success awaits!

Bonus Tip: Consider offering freemium models, where you provide basic content for free and charge for premium features or in-depth content. This allows you to attract a wider audience while still generating income from dedicated fans.

CONCLUSION: MASTERING THE ALGORITHM AND EMBRACING CHANGE

Mastering the X Algorithm: Your Map to Navigating the Digital Jungle

Remember those childhood tales of fearless explorers, trekking through uncharted territories, deciphering ancient maps to uncover hidden treasures? Navigating the X algorithm can feel eerily similar – a quest to understand the hidden rules that govern the digital landscape, a journey to uncover the secrets of visibility and growth. But fear not, algorithmic adventurers! The conclusion of this guide is your compass, pointing you towards mastery of the algorithm and unlocking its potential for your X. success.

Key takeaways from our journey:

- Understand the algorithm's core values: Relevance, engagement, and consistency are the pillars upon which the algorithm stands. Craft content that aligns with these values to increase your visibility.

- Optimize your content: Align with user interests, leverage trending topics, utilize strategic keywords, and craft captivating captions.

- Engage your audience: Respond to comments, participate in conversations, and encourage interactions. Remember, engagement is the lifeblood of the algorithm.

- Post consistently: Regularly share content to maintain a steady presence in the algorithm's eye. Treat consistency as your compass, guiding you through the digital jungle.

- Experiment and analyze: Track your performance, test different strategies, and adapt your approach based on insights. Remember, data is your guide, revealing the paths that lead to success.

Stay Ahead of the Curve: Adapting to Changes and Updates

The algorithm, like any living entity, is constantly evolving. To thrive in this ever-changing landscape, embrace these principles:

- Stay informed: Keep abreast of algorithm updates and trends through official X. sources, industry blogs, and creator communities.

- Adapt your strategies: Be willing to adjust your content and approach based on new insights and changes. Remember, flexibility is your machete, clearing the path through the shifting digital terrain.

- Experiment relentlessly: Never stop testing new ideas and formats. Embrace change as an opportunity to discover new paths to success.

Remember:

- The algorithm is your guide, not your master. Use it to your advantage, but don't let it dictate your creativity.

- Authenticity and passion are your ultimate compass. Stay true to your voice, your values, and your audience, and you'll always find your way.

- The journey to X. success is an ongoing adventure. Embrace the challenges, celebrate the victories, and never stop exploring the possibilities that the platform holds.

Go forth, algorithmic adventurers! Master the algorithm, adapt to its changes, and chart your unique path to success in the ever-evolving world of X. Remember, the treasures you uncover along the way – the connections made, the communities built, and the impact created – will far surpass any fleeting metrics. Now, venture forth, and let your creativity conquer the digital frontier!

BONUS CHAPTERS:
DEEP DIVE FOR X. MASTERS

Welcome, brave adventurers, to the forbidden territory of the Bonus Chapters! Here, we venture beyond the introductory map and delve into the intricate details, the secret strategies, and the real-world case studies that will transform you from X. explorer to X. master. So, tighten your digital belts, sharpen your analytical blades, and prepare to conquer new frontiers of success!

Advanced Strategies for Power Users

This chapter unveils the hidden ninja moves of the X. elite, strategies reserved for those who dare to push the boundaries and unlock the platform's full potential. We'll explore:

- Content hacking techniques: Learn how to leverage trending topics, optimize hashtags, and utilize advanced analytics to skyrocket your content's visibility.

- Collaboration mastery: Discover the art of strategic partnerships, influencer collaborations, and cross-platform promotion to expand your reach and tap into new audiences.

- Monetization beyond the basics: Dive into cutting-edge monetization strategies like live streaming monetization, virtual product sales, and exclusive membership models to diversify your income streams.

- Automation and scheduling tools: Uncover the secrets of time-saving automation tools that streamline your workflow, free up your creative energy, and maximize your efficiency.

Case Studies: Real-World Examples of Success

Theory is powerful, but seeing is believing. In this chapter, we'll dissect the winning strategies of real X. masters, analyzing their content, engagement tactics, and monetization models to provide tangible blueprints for your own success. We'll explore:

- The fitness coach who built a global community: Learn how she combined engaging workout routines, strategic collaborations, and a freemium membership model to attract millions of followers and build a thriving online empire.

- The tech blogger who became an industry authority: Discover how he leveraged in-depth product reviews, data-driven insights, and targeted partnerships to establish himself as a trusted voice in his niche and attract lucrative brand deals.

- The artist who turned her passion into profit: Witness how she transformed her digital artwork into limited-edition digital collectibles, hosted interactive live streams, and fostered a supportive community to create a sustainable and fulfilling career.

Troubleshooting Common Challenges

Even the most seasoned adventurers face obstacles. This chapter equips you with the tools to overcome common X. challenges, such as:

- Low engagement and reach: Discover actionable strategies to boost your visibility, attract new followers, and spark meaningful conversations with your audience.

- Monetization roadblocks: Learn how to overcome income plateaus, identify new revenue streams, and optimize your monetization tactics for maximum profitability.

- Content burnout and creative slumps: Explore effective methods to reignite your creative spark, overcome content fatigue, and consistently produce high-quality content that resonates with your audience.

Remember:

- Mastery is a journey, not a destination. These bonus chapters are just the beginning. Keep learning, keep experimenting, and keep pushing the boundaries of what's possible on X.

- Community is your compass. Surround yourself with other X. enthusiasts, share your challenges and successes, and learn from each other's experiences.

- Never stop exploring. The digital landscape is constantly evolving, so stay curious, embrace change, and be ready to adapt your strategies when needed.

Go forth, X. masters! With these bonus chapters as your guide, you're equipped to conquer the platform, build a thriving online presence, and leave your mark on the digital world. So, raise your virtual flag, embark on your next adventure, and remember, the greatest treasures lie beyond the familiar horizon!